ANSELM GRÜN is a Benedictine monk who has written approximately 300 books that have been translated into 30 languages. He lives in Germany.

GIULIANO FERRI is an Italian illustrator whose work has been published in Italy, the United States, Japan, and England. His books include *The Story of Daniel in the Lions' Den* (Barefoot Books), *Small Camel Follows the Star* (Albert Whitman), *Jonah's Whale,* and *Jesus* (both Eerdmans).

© Verlag Herder GmbH, Freiburg im Breisgau 2012
D-79104 Freiburg
www.herder.de
Originally published in German under the title
Die Legende vom heiligen Nikolaus
by Verlag Herder GmbH, 2012
This English language translation © Laura Watkinson

Published in 2014 by Eerdmans Books for Young Readers,
an imprint of Wm. B. Eerdmans Publishing Co.
2140 Oak Industrial Dr. NE
Grand Rapids, Michigan 49505
P.O. Box 163, Cambridge CB3 9PU U.K.

www.eerdmans.com/youngreaders

Manufactured at Tien Wah Press in Malaysia
in February 2014, first printing

19 18 17 16 15 14   9 8 7 6 5 4 3 2 1

Library of Congress Cataloging-in-Publication Data

Grün, Anselm, author.
[Legende vom Heiligen Nikolaus. English]
The legend of Saint Nicholas / by Anselm Grün; illustrated by Giuliano Ferri;
translated by Laura Watkinson.
pages cm
ISBN 978-0-8028-5434-6
1. Nicholas, Saint, Bishop of Myra — Juvenile literature. I. Ferri, Giuliano, illustrator.
II. Watkinson, Laura, translator. III. Legende vom Heiligen Nikolaus. Translation of:
IV. Title.
BR1720.N46G7813 2014
270.2092 — dc23
2013044478

THE LEGEND OF
SAINT
NICHOLAS

Written by ANSELM GRÜN

Illustrated by GIULIANO FERRI

Translated by LAURA WATKINSON

Eerdmans Books for Young Readers

Grand Rapids, Michigan • Cambridge, U.K.

MANY hundreds of years ago, a devout and virtuous husband and wife lived in the city of Patara. For a long time they had wanted to have children, so they prayed to God and asked him to send them a child. Finally God gave them a son, and they named him Nicholas, which means "victory of the people."

Even when he was a little boy, Nicholas liked to help people who were in need. He prayed to God and listened to the priest's sermons in church. When Nicholas grew up, he decided to become a priest himself. Like Jesus, he wanted to help people and to tell them about God's love.

SADLY, not long after Nicholas had become a priest, his parents died. Nicholas inherited a large fortune, because his mother and father had been very rich. He did not keep the money for himself but shared it with the poor.

One day Nicholas heard about a man who had three daughters. This man was from a noble family, but he was very, very poor. The man had become so desperate that he was going to sell his three daughters as slaves, so that he could feed the rest of the family.

Nicholas could not allow that to happen! So he took a bag of gold and went in secret to the man's house at night. He tossed the bag through a window.

Now the father had enough money to go looking for a husband for his oldest daughter.

A FEW DAYS LATER Nicholas secretly visited
the house again and threw a second bag of gold through the
window. That meant that the second daughter could marry too.

The father, however, had become curious and wanted to
know who was giving gold to his daughters. Some time later,
when Nicholas tossed a third bag of gold through the window,
the sound woke the man. He ran after Nicholas and recognized
him, but Nicholas asked the father not to tell anyone his secret.

The man and his three daughters were overjoyed, and the
family celebrated and had a magnificent wedding feast.

WHEN THE BISHOP of the city of Myra died, the bishops from the surrounding towns came together with the priests to choose a new bishop. But they could not agree. God spoke in a dream to one of the bishops, saying, "Early tomorrow morning before the service, stand watch at the church door. The first man who enters the church should become your new bishop."

The bishop did as God had commanded. As he watched at the door the next morning, Nicholas entered. The bishops and priests took him and placed him on the bishop's throne.

Nicholas was reluctant at first, but there was no point arguing with all those other bishops. So he did as they wanted and became Bishop of Myra.

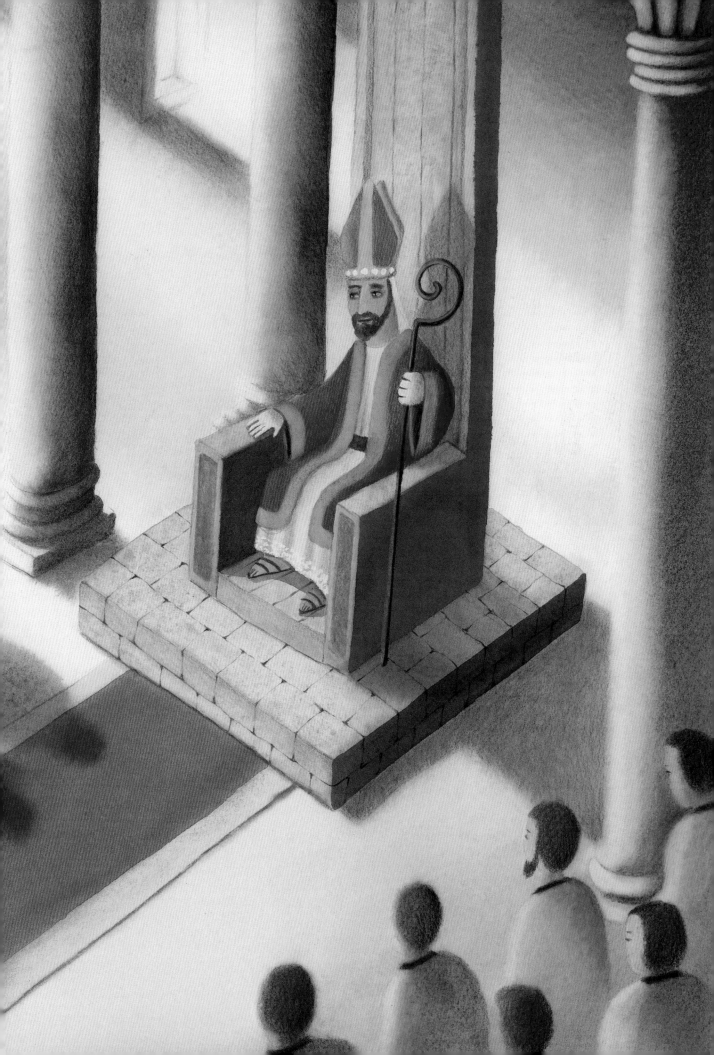

BISHOP NICHOLAS was very popular with the townsfolk of Myra. He helped people whenever he could. He was good and kind, and everyone knew that they could go to him with their worries.

One day some sailors were caught in a bad storm. The waves tossed their ship around, and they thought they were going to sink to the bottom of the sea. In desperation they called out, "Nicholas, if all the good things we have heard about you are true, then please help us too!"

Suddenly the sailors saw Nicholas walking across the sea toward them. He said, "You called me — and here I am."

NICHOLAS climbed up into the ship with the sailors
and helped them with their sails and rudder. Soon the storm
stopped and the sea became calm. Nicholas disappeared as
quickly as he had arrived.

The men sailed their ship safely into the harbor at Myra
and then headed straight for Bishop Nicholas' church, where
they thanked him for saving them. But Nicholas said to them,
"You should not thank me, but God. It is he who saved you."

Since that day, Nicholas has been the patron saint of sailors.

ONCE there was a terrible famine. Not a drop of rain had fallen for a very long time. The sun burned down from the sky and scorched the entire harvest. The people of Myra became very hungry, because there was no grain to be found anywhere in the land.

So they went to Nicholas and asked him for help. Nicholas kneeled down and prayed to God. And God answered him, telling Nicholas to go to the harbor early the next morning.

WHEN NICHOLAS got to the harbor the following morning, a merchant ship from Alexandria had just arrived. It was loaded to the brim with grain for the emperor.

Nicholas went to the ship and asked the captain to give him some grain to help ease the people's suffering. But the captain said, "I'm sorry, but I can't give you anything. The grain has been measured very precisely. If we lose any, the emperor will punish us severely."

But Nicholas promised that not one single grain would be missing when they reached the emperor. So, finally, the captain agreed.

NICHOLAS gave the people as much grain as they needed
from the ship, and they all had enough to eat. There was even some
left to sow for the following year. The terrible famine was over.
Everyone went to Nicholas and thanked him for his help.

When the merchant ship reached the emperor, the captain
found that what Nicholas had said was true: not one single grain was
missing. The sailors told everyone what had happened in Myra. They
praised God and thanked him. The news of the miracle quickly spread
throughout the entire region.

AFTER HIS DEATH, Nicholas was made a saint, and many people remembered him for his kindness.

One time, a nobleman who had no children asked for Saint Nicholas' help so that God would give him a son. The man promised that he would have a golden cup made for the saint if his wish came true. Finally, the nobleman's wife did indeed have a son. The nobleman remembered his promise and had a golden cup made, but it was so beautiful that he decided to keep it for himself. He had another one made for Saint Nicholas instead.

The nobleman and his son set out in a boat to take the cup to the church of Saint Nicholas. On the way, the son used the first cup to scoop some water from the river. But he tumbled into the water, taking the cup with him, and he drowned.

EVEN THOUGH he was mourning his dead son, the father
sailed on to the church of Saint Nicholas so that he could keep his promise.
When he arrived, he placed the second cup on the altar. But it fell over. The
nobleman picked it up again. Once again, it fell and rolled off the altar.
This happened a number of times.

Then the door of the church opened, and the son he had believed
to be dead walked in, holding the first cup in his hand.

The boy placed the cup on the altar — and this time it stayed
where it was. He told his father that it was Saint Nicholas who
had saved him from the water. The man was overjoyed
and placed both cups on the altar for Saint Nicholas.

PEOPLE all over the world love Saint Nicholas because of the many miracles that he performed during his lifetime, and even from heaven after his death.

Because he was such a good friend to children who were in need, young people in some countries still receive gifts on his feast day, December 6. On the evening of December 5, they leave their shoes or a plate by the door and hope that Saint Nicholas will leave something for them. Even today, on the feast of Saint Nicholas, German children like to sing . . .

Let us be glad and full of cheer,
and rejoice in our Lord above.
Happy, happy, tra-la-la-la,
Now St. Nicholas' Eve is here,
now St. Nicholas' Eve is here.